Problem of the Day • 1

How many different number sentences with a sum of 12 can you write? Use the numbers from 0 to 9.

Problem of the Day • 2

Carrie bought some carrots for her horse. She gave her horse 3 carrots on Monday, 2 on Tuesday, and 1 on Wednesday. On Wednesday night, she had 7 carrots left. How many carrots did she buy?

Problem of the Day • 3

An empty elevator went up 3 floors, where 7 people got on. Then it went down 6 floors, where 4 people got on and 6 people got off. Then it went up 10 floors, and 5 people got on and 3 got off. How many people are now on the elevator?

Problem of the Day • 4

Draw 5 triangles using only 10 lines.

Problem of the Day • 5

Tom's locker number is a 2-digit number. The digits add up to 13 but have a difference of 3. What locker numbers could he have?

Problem of the Day • 6

There are 4 brothers. Doug is older than Darren. Doug is younger than Dan. David is the youngest. List the brothers in order from oldest to youngest.

Problem of the Day • 7

Make a number sentence using only the digits 5, 6, 7, and 8 and the operation of addition.

$$? + ? = ? + ?$$

Problem of the Day • 8

Without subtracting, explain how you know which difference is greatest.

$$16 - 8 \quad 16 - 10$$

$$16 - 7 \quad 16 - 9$$

$$16 - 5 \quad 16 - 6$$

Problem of the Day • 9

Jamal has 20¢. Which coins could he have? List as many different combinations as you can.

Problem of the Day • 10

Bob, Jan, Kay, and Lou are in line.

Bob is not first.

Jan is last.

Kay is between Bob and Lou.

Where is Lou?

Problem of the Day • 11

Akemi has a collection of 200 CDs. She wants to buy 5 more CDs each week. How many CDs will she have in 10 weeks?

Problem of the Day • 12

Rico and Ramona are packing their 347 video tapes into boxes. Small boxes hold 10 tapes. Large boxes hold 100 tapes. How many large and small boxes do they need?

Problem of the Day • 13

Tom is thinking of a number. The number has 3 ones, twice as many hundreds, and no tens. What is Tom's number?

Molly is thinking of a number. Her number uses the same digits as Tom's number in a different order. What is Molly's number?

Problem of the Day • 14

If you know a number, is there always a number that would be more than your number? Explain.

Problem of the Day • 15

Pizza for the snack bar is sold in cases of 24. If 20 cases are ordered for the snack bar how many pizzas will that be?

Problem of the Day • 16

What shape could you make if you started with a regular hexagon and cut off 2 triangles?

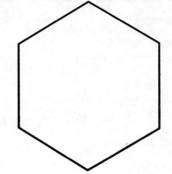

Problem of the Day • 17

I am a 4-digit number with 8 hundreds and 4 ones. The sum of all my digits is 16. What number am I?

Problem of the Day • 18

Nora has 100,900 coins in her collection. If she gets 10 more coins each week, how many will she have after 10 weeks?

Problem of the Day • 19

I am a 6-digit number. Two of my digits are 4. Two of my digits are 0. The other 2 digits are odd numbers with a sum of 8. I am the greatest number you can make with those digits. What number am I?

Problem of the Day • 20

Tito wants to invite Al, Ben, Carl, Dave, and Ed to his house. He can have only two friends at a time. Make a list to show the combinations he could have.

Problem of the Day • 21

The vowels *a, e, i, o,* and *u* are worth four points. All other letters are worth one point. Write a word worth ten points.

Problem of the Day • 22

Find three numbers you can add mentally to get a sum of 201.

Problem of the Day • 23

Louisa is playing a game with her friend. When she says 15, her partner says 20. When she says 8, her partner says 13. When she says 30, her partner says 35. What should her partner say when Louisa says 14? 100?

Problem of the Day • 24

4 and 5 are consecutive numbers. Their sum is 9. Find two consecutive numbers whose sum is 75.

A shower uses about 5 gallons of water a minute. How much water would you use for a 5-minute shower? Estimate how much water you use for showers in a week. A month.

Problem of the Day • 26

Jody, Pat, and Dan each participate in either soccer, swimming, or baseball. Dan doesn't use a ball in his sport. Pat needs a bat for his sport. Match each person with their sport.

Problem of the Day • 27

Draw three more ways that 4 stamps could be attached together.

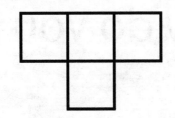

Problem of the Day • 28

After the 5th inning, the score of the game was Blues 1, Reds 4. The final score was 5 to 3. Who won the game? How do you know?

Problem of the Day • 29

If today is Wednesday, what day of the week will it be in 10 days?

Problem of the Day • 30

Twenty of the 14 girls and 15 boys in Mr. Brown's class ride the bus. What is the least number of boys that could ride the bus? Explain.

Problem of the Day • 31

What single coin equals the sum of 5 other coins?

Problem of the Day • 32

There are 27 bones in one hand and wrist. Each arm contains 6 bones. How many bones do you have in both arms, wrists and hands?

Problem of the Day • 33

You have 46¢. You have 4 coins.
Which coins do you have?

Problem of the Day • 34

Tim needs a pair of matching socks. He doesn't want to turn a light on in his room because it would wake his little brother. He has 10 blue socks and 10 brown socks in his drawer. How many socks must he take out of his drawer to be sure he gets a same-colored pair?

Problem of the Day • 35

Ray has 12 pennies. He needs to place them in 3 stacks. Each stack must have a different number of pennies. What is the greatest number of pennies that can be in one stack?

Problem of the Day • 36

What are three different even numbers that add up to 44? Find at least two other sets of even numbers that total 44.

Problem of the Day • 37

May is having a party. She needs chairs for 22 friends. She has tables for 4 and tables for 6. How many of each type of table does she need to seat 22 friends with no empty chairs?

Problem of the Day • 38

A class is divided into 6 teams. Each team has an animal or bird name—Antelope, Bear, Cheetah, Deer, Eagle, or Fox. The first person in line is assigned to the Antelope team, the second person to the Bear team, and so on. Marta is the 38th person in line. Which team will she be on?

Problem of the Day • 39

Marie is twice as old as her cat. In two years Marie will be 10. How old is the cat now?

Problem of the Day • 40

At the fair, the Pet the Animal corral contains 20 animals. For every 4 baby chicks there are 3 kid goats, 2 lambs, and 1 calf. How many of each type of animal are there?

Problem of the Day • 41

Fill in the circles with 1-digit numbers so that the sum of circles next to each other equals the number between them.

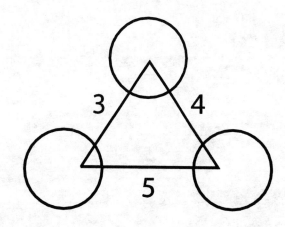

Problem of the Day • 42

There are 4 trees. In each tree there are 6 monkeys. Each monkey is holding 2 bananas. How many bananas are there in all?

Problem of the Day • 43

Mrs. Rand had $75.00. She bought a dress for $39.95 and a pair of shoes for $27.50. Does she have enough money to buy a hat for $6.25? Explain.

Problem of the Day • 44

You have ten minutes to eat lunch. Should you heat a can of soup or make a big pot of soup from fresh ingredients? Explain. What if you had two hours before lunch?

Problem of the Day • 45

Which exercise does not belong?

$$
\begin{array}{cccc}
325 & 325 & 325 & 325 \\
-256 & -108 & -95 & -212 \\
\end{array}
$$

Problem of the Day • 46

I got in line for the Wild Rocket roller coaster at 10:35 A.M. The sign said there was a 20 minute wait from this point, then the ride was 10 minutes long. What time was it when I got off the roller coaster?

Problem of the Day • 47

Shana had $20. She went to two movies on Saturday. The tickets cost $4.50 each. Then she went to a Sunday matinee for $3.00. How much money does she have left?

Problem of the Day • 48

When driving on the turnpike you pay a toll of 35¢ for every 5 miles you drive. If you drive 25 miles, how much money will you owe in tolls?

Problem of the Day • 49

On Monday it rained for a total of one hour and forty-six minutes. First it rained for fifteen minutes and stopped. Then it rained some more. How long did it rain the second time?

Problem of the Day • 50

Jim can swim the 100-meter race in two minutes and the 186-meter race in four minutes. How long should it take for him to swim the 50-meter race? the 800-meter race?

Problem of the Day • 51

Ron's age is double Terri's age. Sally's age is double Ron's age. Ron is 14 years old. How old are Terri and Sally?

Problem of the Day • 52

What patterns do you see? Complete the table.

toys	1	2	3		
batteries	4	8	12		

Problem of the Day • 53

An array is an arrangement of objects in rows and columns. Tell a multiplication story for an array with three rows of four objects.

Problem of the Day • 54

Mrs. Red Cloud bought 4 cards of buttons.
There were 5 buttons on each card.
Did she buy more than 15 buttons?

José and Carlos collect baseball cards.

José has 5 groups of 2 cards.

Carlos has 2 groups of 5 cards.

How many cards do they have together?

Problem of the Day • 56

Sara's travel-decal collection has expanded. She now has double the original number of decals. How will she display them?

Problem of the Day • 57

Tomato sauce comes in 8-ounce cans and 16-ounce cans. How many of either size can should Sarina buy if she needs 32 ounces of tomato sauce?

Problem of the Day • 58

Tony has 3 days of baseball practice during each full week of May. How many days can he practice in May?

Problem of the Day • 59

Emilio and his partner are playing cards with two other friends. Each player gets 5 cards. How many cards do the players have in all?

Problem of the Day • 60

Victor took 7 cartons of binders of stamps to sell at the stamp show. In each carton he had 4 binders filled with stamps. When he came home he had only 23 binders. How many fewer binders did he bring home?

Problem of the Day • 61

Jean writes an odd number. Her number is between 15 and 27. It is a product of 3 and another factor. What could her number be?

Problem of the Day • 62

Mrs. Brown gives the cashier 3 five-dollar bills and a dime. She receives 3 one-dollar bills and 2 quarters in change. How much money did she spend?

Problem of the Day • 63

Rico put 10 marbles into 3 cans. The second can has twice as many marbles as the first can. There are three ways he could have put the marbles in the cans. What are the ways?

Problem of the Day • 64

I'm a 3-digit number. Added to myself, I'm half of one thousand. What number am I?

Problem of the Day • 65

Travis went to sleep at 8:30 P.M.

He woke up at 6:00 A.M.

How long did he sleep?

Problem of the Day • 66

Mitch, Beth, and Carl want to share a giant 24-inch-long sandwich. Mitch wants twice as much as Beth, and Carl wants half as much as Mitch. How much does each person want?

Problem of the Day • 67

There are 4 boxes of shirts. Each box contains 2 shirts. A case contains 6 boxes. How many shirts are in a case?

Peggy has five coins in her pocket. All the coins are smaller than a quarter. Three coins are the same. What is the greatest amount of money she could have in her pocket?

Problem of the Day • 69

Between noon on Saturday and 6 A.M. on Sunday, how many times does the minute hand of a clock pass the hour hand?

Problem of the Day • 70

Mrs. Ross puts the same number of plants in each window box. There are more than 2 but fewer than 5 window boxes, and more than 25 but fewer than 30 plants. How many plants and window boxes could she have?

Problem of the Day • 71

Rita's family spent $16 to go to the fair. An adult ticket costs $5. A child's ticket costs $2. How many children and how many adults went to the fair? Explain.

Problem of the Day • 72

The sum of two numbers is 13.

The product of the two numbers is 36.

What are the two numbers?

Problem of the Day • 73

Joy gave either 6 or 7 marbles to each of 4 friends. What is the fewest number of marbles she could have given away? What is the greatest number?

Problem of the Day • 74

Erin tossed a number cube labeled 1 through 6 three times. The sum of the three tosses was 16. What numbers could she have tossed?

Problem of the Day • 75

Sal has twice as many marbles as Rita. Does Sal have an even number of marbles or an odd number of marbles? How do you know?

Problem of the Day • 76

There are 3 feet in a yard. Mrs. Wilson needs 9 yards of wire for the rabbit hutch she is building. She has 25 feet of wire. How much more wire does she need?

Problem of the Day • 77

The library charges 10¢ each day for an overdue children's book and 25¢ each day for an overdue adult book. Mr. Molina paid $1.05 for 6 books that were one day late. How many children's books and how many adult books did he have?

Problem of the Day • 78

Max has a jar with blue marbles and green marbles. If he closes his eyes and takes out 3 marbles, how many different combinations of colors of marbles could he have?

Problem of the Day • 79

Jesse has less than 20 guinea pigs. If he puts 4 guinea pigs in each cage, he has 3 left over. If he puts 5 guinea pigs in each cage, he has 1 guinea pig left over. How many guinea pigs does he have?

Problem of the Day • 80

Kyle planted 25 sunflower seeds. Out of every 5 seeds he planted, 3 seeds grew into plants. How many of the 25 seeds grew into plants?

Problem of the Day • 81

Karen's birthday is the 3rd day of March. Lynn's birthday is the 5th day of May. How many days apart are their birthdays?

Problem of the Day • 82

I am between 1 and 30. If I am multiplied by myself, the product is 49. What number am I?

Problem of the Day • 83

I have 45¢ worth of coins in my pocket. What is the least number of coins I can have? List the coins.

Problem of the Day • 84

Look for a pattern. Write the rule, and give the next 3 numbers in the pattern. 3, 8, 13, 18,...

My bedtime is 8:30 P.M. I slept until 7:00 A.M.
How long did I sleep?

Problem of the Day • 86

The product of the digits in the mystery number is 24; it is an even number; and it is greater than 23 × 9.

Find the mystery number from the group below:

346   240   138

226   423   641

Problem of the Day • 87

Lisa and Lynn are twins. Mike and Mark are twins. The girls are 2 years older than the boys. The sum of all their ages is 40. How old is each person?

Problem of the Day • 88

There are 60 seconds in a minute. What activity might you do for 600 seconds? for 6,000 seconds?

Problem of the Day • 89

Find a different number for each shape so that:

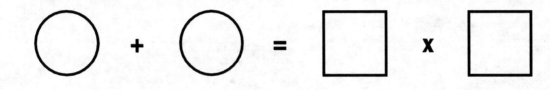

Problem of the Day • 90

A piece of fabric is shaped like a rectangle. The perimeter of the fabric is 10 meters. The length is 4 meters. What is the width? What is the area?

Problem of the Day • 91

Andrew used 40 posts to fence in his rectangular garden. There were 14 posts on each long side. How many posts were on each short side? Explain.

For breakfast Max said he had a cylinder full of white liquid, the inside of a sphere, a rectangular prism with jam, and half a sphere of some flakes. What do you think he had for breakfast?

Students are asked to use no more than 15 shapes to make a picture. Joey made a picture using twice as many circles as squares. He used three times as many triangles as squares. How many shapes did he use in all?

Erin used toothpicks to make examples of polygons. She used one toothpick for each side of a polygon. She made a triangle, a square, a pentagon, and a hexagon. How many toothpicks did she use?

Problem of the Day • 95

There are 24 students in Mr. Howard's class. Ten students have dogs, 4 students have hamsters, 8 students have cats, and 2 students have birds. Does every student in the class have a pet?

Problem of the Day • 96

There are 7 coins in a row. The first is a quarter, the second is a dime, the third is a quarter, the fourth is a dime. The pattern continues. What is the value of the row of coins?

Megan, Nathan, and Rosa went shopping. Together, Megan and Nathan spent $8. Together, Nathan and Rosa spent $9. Megan and Rosa spent $11 together. How much did each person spend?

Mark, Bill, Tony, and Kim each played one game of dominoes against each of the others. How many games were played?

Problem of the Day • 99

How many ordered pairs do you have for a grid that goes from 0 to 5 in both directions?

Problem of the Day • 100

For a display, Mr. Brown stacks cans of peaches so that each row has 1 less can than the row below. The top row of his display has one can and there are 6 rows of cans. How many cans does he use in the display?

Problem of the Day • 101

June has 30 days, July has 31 days, and August has 31 days. Is the sum of these days even or odd?

Problem of the Day • 102

In three days, 2 chickens laid 5 eggs. How many eggs will 6 chickens lay in six days?

Problem of the Day • 103

Enrique has 9 coins that add up to 50¢. He has an odd number each of quarters, dimes, and pennies. He has an even number of nickels. How many of each coin does he have?

Problem of the Day • 104

Morgan needs $\frac{6}{8}$ yard of yarn to make hair for her puppet. Karen gives Megan $\frac{3}{4}$ yard of yarn. Does Megan have enough yarn? Explain.

Problem of the Day • 105

Penny, John, and Helga are sharing a pizza. Penny has $\frac{1}{6}$ of the pizza, John has $\frac{1}{2}$, and Helga has $\frac{1}{3}$. Who has the largest share of the pizza?

Problem of the Day • 106

On Monday half of Mr. Wilson's class bought a carton of milk at lunch. If 18 students bought milk, how many students are in Mr. Wilson's class?

Alexander says that $3\frac{1}{2}$ pizzas were eaten at the last Math Team meeting. Alicia says that 28 pieces of pizza were eaten at that same meeting. How can they both be right?

Problem of the Day • 108

The perimeter of Mr. Wang's garden is 56 feet. If the garden is 10 feet wide, what is the length of the garden?

Problem of the Day • 109

How many different 3-digit whole numbers can be written using the digits 2, 4, and 8? The digits can be used once.

Amy and Philip made place mats for the school craft fair. Amy says she sold twice as many as Philip. Philip says he sold half of all the place mats he made. Amy sold 12 place mats. How many did Philip make?

Michelle had a dozen eggs. She used three eggs baking a cake. After accidentally dropping two eggs, she bought another half-dozen at the store. How many eggs does Michelle have now?

Problem of the Day • 112

A month of the year is chosen at random. What is the probability that it has 31 days?

Problem of the Day • 113

A mother is 6 times as old as her son. In 20 years she will be twice as old as her son. How old are they now?

Problem of the Day • 114

On Monday both Rosa and Paul ate waffles for breakfast. Rosa has waffles for breakfast every other day. Paul has waffles for breakfast every third day. On what day of the week will they both eat waffles next?

Problem of the Day • 115

Ruth is writing a story about dogs and birds. She says there are 5 heads and 14 feet in her story. How many dogs and how many birds are in her story?

Problem of the Day • 116

Melissa needs 36 quilt squares to make a quilt. She makes 1 quilt square the first day, 2 squares the second day, 3 squares the third. She continues in this pattern until she has all 36 squares. How many days does it take her to make all the squares?

Problem of the Day • 117

A slice of bread has the same number of calories as 3 carrots. One ice cream bar with chocolate coating has the same number of calories as 12 carrots. How many slices of bread have the same number of calories as the ice cream bar?

Problem of the Day • 118

The sum of two numbers is 28. The product of the numbers is 147. The difference of the numbers is 14. When you divide the greater number by the lesser number, the quotient is 3. What are the numbers?

Problem of the Day • 119

Mrs. Rodriquez uses 6 quarters for each load of laundry. At the bank, she changes $20 into quarters. How many loads of laundry can she do? How many quarters will be left over?

Problem of the Day • 120

Wanda fills orders for widgets at the Widget Works factory. She uses 4 boxes to pack up 23 widgets and 9 boxes to pack up 51 widgets. What is the greatest number of widgets she can pack in each box?